ARTHUR, THE AMAZING MANTIS

ARTHUR, THE AMAZING MANTIS
A STORY OF UNEXPECTED CONNECTION

by
ELSA KENDALL

A Stories from the Natural World Book

ARTHUR, THE AMAZING MANTIS
A Story of Unexpected Connection

If you'd like to stay in touch, please visit
www.storiesfromthenaturalworld.mysojournal.com.

THIS IS THE STORY about a relationship between an insect and a human being. It is a story of serendipity and delight, respect and wonder, and the ultimate understanding that we are all truly connected by a mysterious, sacred web.

IT WAS THE FIRST OF OCTOBER, a lovely, mild, early autumn day. My neighbor, Zoe, and I were standing under the portal near my front door, chatting. Her kitty, Emma, was lounging against the wall, happy to be outside. Suddenly, in the middle of our conversation, something white dropped from above, right at my feet. The startled kitty went to see what had fallen.

"Look, Zoe," I said, "it's a praying mantis. It's so pale. I've never seen one like that before." Zoe scooped Emma up to keep the insect safe from her, and we watched as the mantis righted itself and began to climb up the wall. It looked fine, despite having dropped from so high.

I went inside to get my camera so I could photograph it. Speaking softly, I told it how beautiful it was. As it climbed, it would stop and look over its shoulder at me with big, compound eyes, the tiny pinhole pupils staring steadily

as it put one leg
ever so slowly in
front of another.
I wondered how it
saw me, a giant of
a being compared
to its little self.

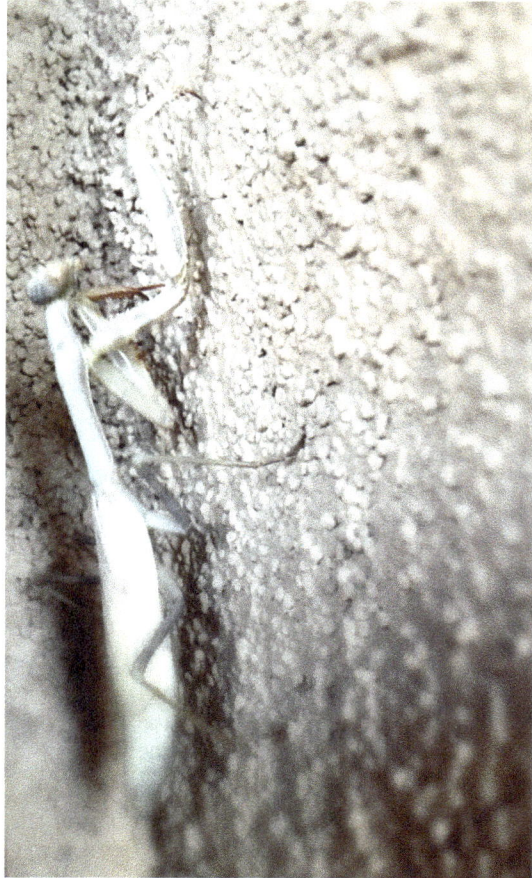

Zoe and I chatted for a while longer and then she said goodbye, taking kitty and leaving me to this little creature. I made some more photos, and I said goodbye and how lovely it was to meet. "Perhaps I'll see you later, little one," I whispered as I went into the house.

Later, I was at the open kitchen window, looking through the screen at nothing in particular. Just then, I noticed a tiny hand coming over the window ledge, then a foreleg, then the entire leg, and then a head.

It was the pale, pale mantis.

It stopped and looked at me through the screen.

"Hello," I said. The mantis had made its way several feet from where I'd left it, walking past the front door, up the wall, over the window ledge, and up onto the window screen. "Hi, little buddy. How'd you get here so fast?"

It continued to walk up the screen. Up, up, up. This little one was very curious. And it really seemed to respond to my speaking, even coming to meet me at eye level. We regarded one another for a bit, and I noticed what a wonderful climber it was—very slow and very deliberate.

It had been a while since I'd been in the
company of any creature, and it was lovely
to have a little being in my orbit. I carried on
with my day and thought I probably wouldn't
see it again.

The next morning I stepped out of the front door. Sipping my tea, I leaned against the portal post, enjoying the sun's warmth upon my face. Soon I became aware of something, a presence, behind me. I turned to look. Below the kitchen window a tan faucet protruded from the wall, fully bathed in the early morning sun. Hanging upside down from the faucet was the mantis. It, too, seemed to be enjoying the sunshine.

I sat down on the ground next to it and marveled how its color had changed slightly, the paleness now blended into a warm tan, matching the color upon which it was sitting.

"Hi, Arthur." I had no idea where this name had come from, but it seemed to fit. Once again he regarded me with his enormous eyes, turning his head from side to side as I sat down on the ground to speak to him. He seemed to like the company and the quiet of the morning, as I did.

We sat for a while enjoying the sun together. After some time, my neighbor, Rita, came outside. "Hey, whaddaya doin' there?" she asked me. "Come see," I said.

Rita was ninety-two years old, a short little pistol of a woman, originally from the Bronx. She had a fidgety, nervous energy and spoke in a loud voice. She saw me sitting on the ground talking to . . .

an insect.

Walking over, she repeated, "Whaddaya doin'?"

I pointed to the mantis. "This little guy fell from the portal ceiling yesterday, and he's been here ever since."

"He? How d'you know it's a male?" And I told her I thought that male mantises are smaller, and he seemed pretty small to me.

Just then I noticed Arthur becoming a little agitated. He repositioned himself a few times and walked around the faucet, fixing his eyes upon us. Suddenly he slipped and fell to the ground below, landing on a green hose. I watched him try to pull himself back up, but it was too slippery.

23

I wanted to help Arthur, but he was so delicate I was afraid to touch him in case it might hurt him.

"Could you maybe get a small stick and help him that way?" Rita asked.

"No, it might hurt him. I think I'll just let Arthur find his own way."

"Arthur? That's his name?" asked Rita.

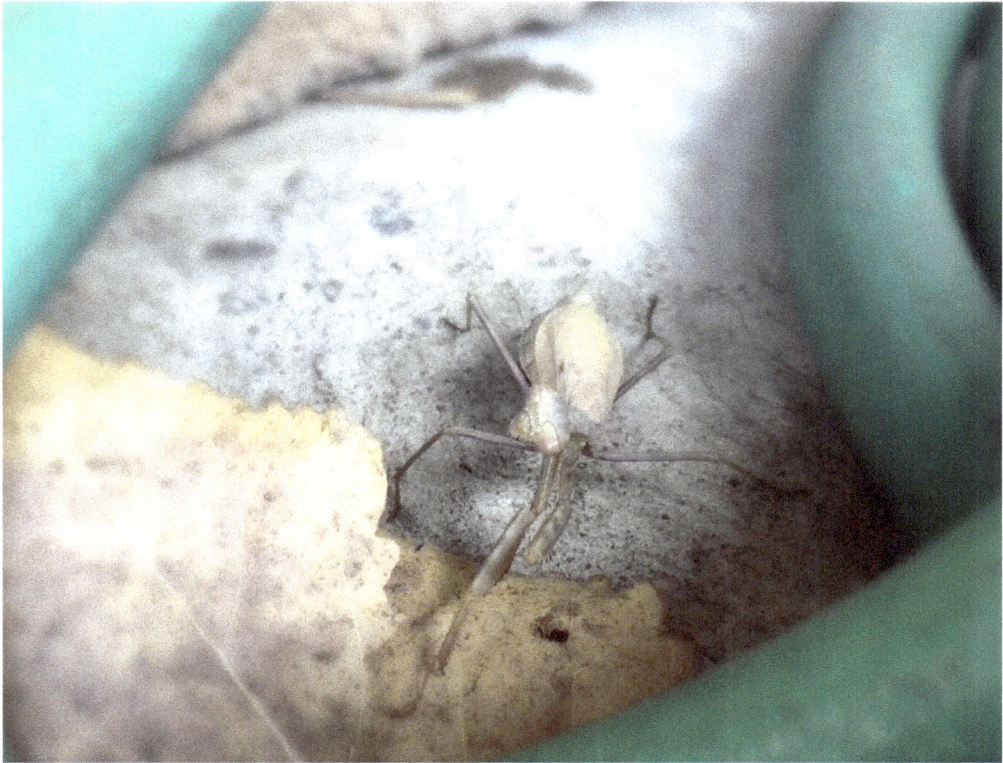

I smiled at her. "Yes, that's his name." And I began to talk to him some more. Rita thought this was funny, my talking to a praying mantis. "I have to go. Tell me what he answers," she called over her shoulder, chuckling as she closed the door.

Arthur and I continued being there together. I sat quietly next to him, observing his slow and steady movement. He seemed to feel me and that I was gentle.

Over the next few days I photographed
Arthur, and I made a video of him. I hung out
with him. It was nice for both of us. Peaceful. I
noticed how perfectly his legs were made, how the
front ones could wrap around as they grasped
something. How he had two sets of back legs,
each with a tiny foot. How his wings folded like
an envelope against his abdomen. I wondered if
he had used those wings to break his fall when
he'd tumbled from the ceiling.

The next day I left for work. There he was again, on the faucet, blending in very well. I leaned down very close to him. He looked right at me. "See you later, Arthur," I whispered, and walked to my car.

31

Several hours later, I came home. Arthur wasn't where I'd last seen him. "He must have gone," I thought, looking around my front door and feeling a little sad. I had become used to his presence and missed seeing him.

Then, a bit later, there he was! He'd climbed the screen again to see me in the kitchen making dinner. I even opened the front door to see if he wanted to come in, but he didn't. He liked it outside.

34

This went on for several days. Several days turned into a few weeks, just over three to be exact. I noticed he liked to be close to the house, on the wall, on the screen. Maybe it was warm there for him as the days were becoming cooler.

I never once saw him go past the concrete path where the portal roof ended above. He never went near the large patch of jagged juniper across from my door. He would hover at the edge of it, perhaps waiting for a small bug. But he never went into that jungle. Maybe he knew mice and big spiders lived in there.

I liked Arthur's company. Over the weeks
we developed a real bond. I would sit with him,
not thinking, just watching. Sometimes I would
make photos, and sometimes I'd talk to him. But
usually we just sat quietly together.

It was nearly the end of October, and it was
beginning to get cold. I wondered how Arthur
would survive the winter.

One morning I awakened and went out to see him. He wasn't in any of his usual places. I looked down and there he was, right next to the front door by a little wooden chest that had long, spindly legs. He was crouched on the concrete a few inches from one of these legs, and I sat down to be with him. He seemed odd, not like he usually was. Perhaps the cold was getting to him.

I went into the house and came out later to see him in the same place. But this time he was standing up on his back legs, vertically aligned and pressed against the leg of the chest, holding onto it with his forelegs. I watched him for a minute. "That's so odd," I thought, "I wonder what he's doing." And I went back inside.

When I came out again, half an hour had passed. I found him about a foot away on his back, covered in a sticky spider's web. "Oh, no!" I said out loud. "Arthur, are you okay?"

Taking an aspen leaf from nearby, I knelt down and used the stem to gently pull the web away from him. Righting him, I thought he seemed a little groggy. I lay down next to him and reached out.

He slowly crawled toward me and climbed onto the back of my hand, his tiny feet traversing my warm skin. It tickled. He was the lightest thing I'd ever felt. "Arthur," I said, "I really hope you're okay." He made it across my hand and down to the concrete again. I left him near the front door and went inside.

I wondered why he was standing upright like that. Curious, I went online and looked up "praying mantis." There were lots of photos, so many types of mantises in many colors and sizes, hundreds of them.

And then I saw it, a picture of a green praying mantis standing upright against a thick stem. I read the caption: "The female will stand upright to lay her eggs. The sac is laid against a plant stem, its spongy exterior keeping the eggs safe through the winter until the following spring."

What?

Is that what Arthur was doing, laying eggs?

So he wasn't a "he," he was a "she"? Arthur
was a female praying mantis! All of these days
she'd been waiting for the perfect time and place
to lay her eggs (which is actually one egg sac,
called an ootheca, full of tiny nymph mantises).
But honestly, I didn't know if she'd found the
perfect place.

I looked more closely at the table leg she had been leaning against. Sure enough, in the crack at the base of the leg, there was a tiny sac that appeared to be spongy.

Perhaps feeling the urgency of autumn and the need to release her egg sac, she had decided that the only safe place was next to my front door.

There really wasn't an ideal place for her to lay it. Laid in the juniper patch, it probably wouldn't have been safe. A spider or a mouse could view it as food.

I felt Arthur had entrusted her unborn to me. I needed to protect them. Taking rocks from nearby, I built a fortress around the sac with weighty stones and used others to wedge against the cabinet legs, acting as a brace. I put a note on top asking it not be moved.

Arthur lay still. I imagined she'd used a lot of energy to lay her egg sac, and she needed to rest. I went inside to do some things. As it was a mild day, I left the front door open and the screen door ajar.

By the time I went outside an hour later, she had crawled under the screen door and was on her back. Her body seemed to be drying up. Gone was the translucent exoskeleton. Instead, she was becoming brown and brittle.

With great sadness, I realized she was dying. I lay down next to her and put my hand close by. I talked to Arthur gently, assuring her I would look after her unborn. I would do my best to protect them so they could hatch in the spring.

Tears rolled down my cheeks. I was sad, sad for the loss of this little being with whom I'd shared such a wondrous connection. I was also deeply moved by the beauty of nature, how everything has a rhythm of birth and death and rebirth, and how we are connected to every other living thing.

Arthur had chosen to spend her last month with me. I'd like to think she'd felt safe enough to leave the thing most precious to her, her egg sac, in my care. Her destiny as a female mantis was to carry her unborn and lay them, contained, and in a safe place away from predators, thus ensuring there would be more mantises in the spring. She had done that. Her work was complete. She could leave now.

Arthur was very weak and barely responsive. To insulate her from the cold concrete, I gently slid her onto a postcard I'd found.

It took about a day for her to complete her life journey. I was with her right at the end. The life force left and her body became still. I could feel she had gone. There was an emptiness.

Arthur had been a wonderful companion, and I was sad she had died. Yet, in the sadness, I also felt a sense of wonder. I was deeply grateful for the connection we had shared.

Arthur was much more than a bug. She was a being. And it was her being and my being that had connected, no matter how we looked to each other on the outside.

I will always be grateful Arthur tumbled into my life. She taught me how to become still, to observe and marvel, to sit and just be, content in the quiet with another.

She was delicate, with a perfectly designed body, complex and beautiful, a tiny, mighty force of nature.

APPRECIATION

With gratitude to Oonagh Elisa Hurley for her sensitive editing suggestions. Also to Angela Werneke for her Slimtype suggestion, and for illustrating the wonderful animal Medicine Cards. I am deeply grateful to Janet Elder, whose generosity and editing prowess helped hone this story.

DEDICATION

This book is dedicated to Jeanne Be, whose connection to the natural world and its deities seemed to pulse through every pore of her being. She showered her light and warmth upon me and so many others.

And to Carolyn S, whose laughter was like sunshine. She loved the natural world and all the adventures it brought to her.

ABOUT THE AUTHOR

Elsa Kendall began photographing and writing stories at the age of seven. Her love of nature was inspired by her maternal grandparents, who lived on a small farm in rural New Jersey. Her grandfather kept bees, planted trees, tended an orchard, and created a large, abundant vegetable garden, despite frequent visits from deer and rabbits. Elsa has felt connected to the natural world all her life. She makes her home in the mountains of Northern New Mexico, where it is not unusual for a bear or cougar to sleep under a magical tree called Clementine in her small urban garden.

Arthur, The Amazing Mantis is also available as an ebook from Apple Books, Google Play Books, and KOBO Books.

TO RECEIVE A FREE AUDIO VERSION OF THIS BOOK, visit ArthurAmazingMantis.MySojournal.com.

Stories from the Natural World is a series published by MySojournal Media.

MySojournal™

518 Old Santa Fe Trail, Ste. 1 Santa Fe, NM 87505 U.S.A.

Sign up for subscriber specials here:
www.storiesfromthenaturalworld.mysojournal.com.

Arthur, The Amazing Mantis: A Story of Unexpected Connection

Hardcover ISBN 978-1-7374288-1-7

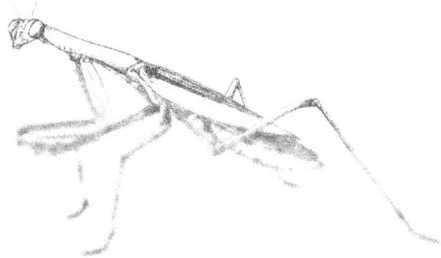